Your Life Matters

Deborah Franklin

Copyright ©2024 by Deborah Franklin

Printed in the United States of America

ALL RIGHTS RESERVED

All rights reserved. No portion of this book may be reproduced in any form without the written permission from the author.

Scriptures marked HCSB are taken from the HOLMAN CHRISTIAN STANDARD BIBLE

(HCSB): Scripture taken from the HOLMAN CHRISTIAN STANDARD BIBLE, copyright© 1999, 2000, 2002, 2003 by Holman Bible Publishers, Nashville Tennessee. All rights reserved.

Scriptures marked AMP are taken from the AMPLIFIED BIBLE (AMP): Scripture taken from the AMPLIFIED® BIBLE, Copyright © 1954, 1958, 1962, 1964, 1965, 1987 by the Lockman Foundation Used by Permission. (www.Lockman.org)

Scriptures marked NKJV are taken from the NEW KING JAMES VERSION (NKJV): Scripture taken from the NEW KING JAMES VERSION®. Copyright© 1982 by Thomas Nelson, Inc. Used by permission. All rights reserved.

Scriptures marked KJV are taken from the KING JAMES VERSION (KJV): KING JAMES VERSION, public domain. Scriptures marked NKJV are taken from the NEW KING JAMES VERSION (NKJV): Scripture taken from the NEW KING JAMES VERSION®. Copyright© 1982 by Thomas Nelson, Inc. Used by permission. All rights reserved.

Scriptures marked ESV are taken from the THE HOLY BIBLE, ENGLISH STANDARD VERSION (ESV): Scriptures taken from THE HOLY BIBLE, ENGLISH STANDARD VERSION ® Copyright© 2001 by Crossway, a publishing ministry of Good News Publishers. Used by permission.

Scriptures marked NCV are taken from the NEW CENTURY VERSION (NCV): Scripture taken from the NEW CENTURY VERSION®. Copyright© 2005 by Thomas Nelson, Inc. Used by permission. All rights reserved.

Published by ReachONE Consulting Services

Dedication

❖ *This page is dedicated to all the people who lost loved ones or friends to suicide. May your hearts be filled with the love of God during your time of grief. May you feel the peace of God as you reach out to Him during your time of need.*

❖ *This book is also dedicated to those who struggle with suicide ideation or have attempted suicide and lived to tell your story. Trust God in the difficult moments and release the pain from your heart. You can have your hope restored. Your life matters!*

Table of Contents

Chapter One 7
    Hopeless Feeling

Chapter Two 13
    Heavy Burdens

Chapter Three 17
    Anxiety Driven Life

Chapter Four 21
    Health Battles

Chapter Five 25
    Isolation

Chapter Six 29
    Extreme Loss

Chapter Seven 35
    Toxic Media

Chapter Eight 39
    Get Active Again

Chapter Nine 43

   Your Purpose

Chapter Ten 47

   True Friends

A Prayer 51

Chapter One
Hopeless Feeling

I remember when I was a young child near age 12. As a child I grew up in financial hardship and I worried about my future all the time. I hated my life and felt I was being punished in some way. I lived in fear and anxiety about everything. My mind was plagued with thoughts about what life would be like if I no longer existed. *Surely, I believed this was the easy way out of daily misery.* I sat on the ledge in a window looking down at the ground and thinking of how

I could quickly die and be free from sadness and internal pain. Although my window was only about two stories high, I thought of jumping out the window to hurt myself and hoping it would result in death.

    Some of you can relate to feeling hopeless. You woke up thinking why do I have to endure another day of pain? Who really cares about me? No one loves me. If I die, then I will no longer be a burden to my family. These thoughts are destructive to your mind. In fact, there are people who care about you and love you. Sometimes God will send people who are not family across your path to lift your spirits when you are feeling down.

    Hopelessness happens to the educated, uneducated, wealthy, poor and even to famous people. In your time of distress, you may feel that you are the only one out there who is struggling on the inside. Go to the scriptures for a moment. In the Bible there is a man named Elijah. In fact, he was a powerful prophet used by God but right after a moment of victory he got very afraid and discouraged and wanted to die. Elijah makes an unusual request to God after learning that his life was in danger. He celebrated a great victory and annihilated the false prophets that were turning people's hearts away from God. He received word that Jezebel, a wicked ruler, put a death threat out on him. Elijah retreated into the wilderness in fear for his life.

1 Kings 19:4 (ESV) says," But he himself went a day's journey into the wilderness and came and sat down under a broom tree. And he asked that he might die, saying, 'It is enough; now, O Lord, take my life, for I am no better than my fathers (ancestors)." After such a great victory, what would make a person concede to defeat? Elijah did not see any hope of being saved from this death threat, so he felt the best solution was for God to take him at that moment.

I remember as a child praying for God to take me out of such an evil and heartless world, but I noticed I always woke up the next day. I wondered if there was more that I could not see and if I allowed the troubles in life to deceive me into thinking that life was not worth living. You may have been in a situation where you felt that the only way out was death. I am here to tell you that if the Lord stopped your suicide attempt, you were saved for a greater purpose in life.

You see, many of us have experienced distress that became so heavy and unbearable. You were never meant to carry that heavy load alone. Think about it. God loves you enough to take all the burdens off your shoulders right now. First you must be willing to surrender it all. Stop trying to figure out how your life will get better. Stop looking for people to fill the emptiness that you feel inside. Maybe you have said all this God stuff is too crazy. I challenge you to come into my world as you read this book and reconsider and take a journey with me as I use the scriptures as a foundation to instill hope again.

I could not save myself. I was a child in so much distress and I badly wanted relief! I know you are reading this book because you want the pain to stop. You are tired of wearing a happy mask just to get along with people. Be real for a moment. Let out this pain. Scream. Cry. Release it because it has been too much to hold on to. I don't care what your background is God sent his son Jesus Christ to die for all of us and to give us the gift of salvation. Salvation is something you do not have to work for. You cannot purchase it. You receive it by faith. Some of you turned to destructive behaviors to numb the pain on the inside but it is no longer working. Your behavior has led to some strong unhealthy habits. Some of you struggle with addictions. Addictions can be with food, gambling, social media, status, drugs, sex, pornography, work, or even people. This is not a conclusive list. Addictions can cause setbacks and even destroy your purpose in life.

There is good news about the prophet Elijah. He did not die before his time. Elijah did not realize that he was weary after fighting in a major battle. An angel visited him and fed him some food which allowed this prophet to regain the needed strength for the next journey (1 Kings 19:5-9). Elijah needed a recharge to keep going. What about you?

Your Life Matters

God's Promise

Jeremiah 29:11 (CSB)

For I know the plans I have for you—this is the Lord's declaration—plans for your well-being, not for disaster, to give you a future and a hope.

Chapter Two
Heavy Burdens

Many of you reading this became overwhelmed by the problems you are facing. Some of you are accustomed to being the strong one in your family. Everyone comes to you for everything. In fact, you became the crisis center for others, but to your own detriment. What am I saying to you? I'll tell you frankly. **LET GO.** Yes, let go of those heavy rocks that you are carrying. One rock can lead to a pile of rocks which then transforms to a mountain. Who made you God? No one! Why are you allowing all these burdens in your life and trying to solve them on your own? It is not possible to fix everyone.

This is a destructive mindset to adopt. This alone can make people feel suicidal. Dump this load on God. Some of you are reading this saying "God can't help me". Allow me to disagree with your statement. YES, God can and will help you if you choose to let go. We can be our own worst enemy in tough times. It is easy to create unrealistic expectations of yourself. You cannot make it in life trying to solve every problem and do everything on your own. Release the things that are beyond your control. Some of you tried to control situations and people far too long and it has created a heavy burden in your life.

It is time to focus on yourself and get mentally well. You have opened too many doors that led to frustration, anger, and severe depression. The burdens you are carrying have created anxiety and even deep resentment toward others you care about. You may be thinking, how does this author know this about me? ***I lived it! Those burdens are false burdens.*** It is not your responsibility to make other people happy. Do you really desire to be free? Then again, I said to release things you have been carrying. These burdens have kept you up in the midnight hours and robbed you of the joy of living in the present.

Who cares what someone may think about you letting go? You are saving your life today. Enough is enough. Say this out loud. **_Enough is enough!_** Something must change now. People who are givers in their family often do not realize they need help themselves. This creates unhealthy codependent relationships which can quickly become very toxic. Give those burdens to the Lord. He can handle everything and every person if you would take a leap of faith and just let go. Do it to heal your heart. You deserve to be free, and you can. Turn off the television—especially the toxic programs. They only fill your heart with more unstable emotions like anxiety. Trust God who can fill your heart with peace and joy. Stop being a control freak.

God's Promise

1 Peter 5: 6-7 (AMP)

Therefore humble yourselves under the mighty hand of God [set aside self-righteous pride], so that He may exalt you [to a place of honor in His Service] at the appropriate time, casting all your cares [all your anxieties, all your worries, and all your concerns, once and for all] on Him, for He cares about you [with deepest affection, and watches over you very carefully].

Chapter Three
Anxiety Driven Life

What are you worrying about? Excessive worry leads to anxiety. You are not a nice person in this state of mind. People will avoid you when they see you coming. Your anxiety filled life can become overwhelming to others. Take a moment and think about what has been stressing you out. What has changed the way you see yourself or how you live in this present world? Have you ever been called a "worry wart"? Let me define this for you. A worry wart is a name given to a person who worries about everything which robs them of the opportunity to enjoy anything. This type of person is miserable internally and is fearful of everything.

If you are not intentional about reprogramming what you think about, your thought life can make you feel insane. Worry warts think like this: "Oh I just got a new car. What if someone hits and totals my car? Then I cannot get to work. If I cannot get to work, then my boss will fire me. Once my boss fires me, I will become homeless. After being homeless my life could be in danger on the streets. Then someone may kill me. My life is worthless."

None of this, I repeat **NONE** of this has happened, but the anxiety filled person will constantly live in their heads because of worry. These thoughts can lead to actual health issues. Are you suffering from panic attacks? Night terrors? Headaches, back aches, stomach aches? Or maybe you had a heart attack from stress and the doctor told you to rest. STOP. I need you to break the habits of worry, but you need God's help because you have lost your peace. The anxiety filled life is not full of peace, but it is a very confused state to be in. Maybe your personal needs were not adequately met as a child, and you adopted a life of worry to ensure that you are always careful about what you do or the places you go.

The fact is no one can control everything that happens, but we can control **HOW** we respond. Some people lived in high anxiety during the COVID pandemic and became compulsive shoppers because they were afraid of running out of food and personal items. Some of you overstocked your shelves and became hoarders! Others were very careful about their food intake and decided to adopt new eating and exercise habits to get healthy. Some were afraid of people and became recluses and never returned to work. Some people decided to live *off the grid* in hopes to gain peace from crime ridden areas and avoided the city life. Unfortunately, some felt hopeless and chose to end their lives. Do not be deceived. There is nothing healthy about worrying about every aspect of your life.

God's Promise

Matthew 6:33 (NKJV)

31 "Therefore do not worry, saying, 'What shall we eat?' or 'What shall we drink?' or 'What shall we wear?' 32 For after all these things the Gentiles seek. For your heavenly Father knows that you need all these things. 33 But seek first the kingdom of God and His righteousness, and all these things shall be added to you.

Chapter Four
Health Battles

There is a familiar phrase that says **health is wealth**. Sometimes dealing with major health issues can lead to depression. As I mentioned earlier, living in anxiety can also cause health problems. As you are aware there are some people who support the practice of physician-assisted suicide. There are times where a terminally ill person loses the desire to live. I am not sure where you stand on this issue, but I firmly believe your life matters even if you are facing a major health crisis right now. You were created for a purpose. If you are currently struggling with a major illness, I pray that you can find joy in the simple things such as waking up, talking, breathing, and having a bed to sleep in.

It is very hard to walk through a major illness with no support from family and friends. I remember being impacted by people who suffered from major health issues within my family. Some were at peace while others were in distress. If you are suffering from a major illness, I want to provide hope by encouraging you right now. I pray that today you will release anything in your heart that has made you bitter about your health problems. Holding bitterness can cause emotional and physical sickness. Take a short inventory of your life. Can you remember when you last smiled? Laughed? Who are the people who walked with you during your darkest times? If they are still around, I encourage you to reach out to them and express your deepest needs or gratitude for their support. It is so amazing to live in a spirit of gratitude.

Never underestimate the power of a kind word, a prayer or even a genuine hug. These actions can heal a wounded soul. Stop and take a deep breath. Think about how you want to spend the next moment. Use this time as a reflective opportunity to count your blessings. I am not trivializing your pain but simply admonishing you to see the beauty in the day that you were blessed to see. If you are prone to pushing people away when you are suffering, welcome them in this space. Your life still matters. Be kind to yourself. You can find joy amid suffering. Tell yourself you will live again. You will laugh again. You will love again. You will find hope again. It is not over.

atively
God's Promise

3 John 1: 2 (KJV)

---

² Beloved, I pray that you may prosper in all things and be in health, just as your soul prospers.

Chapter Five
Isolation

When you are feeling hopeless or down, it is so easy to isolate yourself from people. In fact, you may not want to be around people, but the interaction from loved ones can change your mood. Perhaps you may be embarrassed at times because you are normally a cheerful person. Regardless of the situation, reach out to someone you trust even if it is only one person.

The Centers for Disease Controls and Prevention pointed out that isolation and loneliness can be linked to heart disease, dementia, and even self-harm. Once again there is a direct correlation with our emotions and our physical well-being. Maybe you don't trust people with your problems, but I need you to take a bold step and reach out even if it is a mental health hotline. Humans were created to live in community.

Life can be so much better when you have strong healthy relationships with people. Prolonged isolation can feel like solitary confinement. Maybe you struggle with being vulnerable to people when you are at your weakest. Pick up the phone and at least talk to someone. Some of you isolated because you were deeply hurt by people you trusted in childhood. Maybe you just left a harmful or an abusive relationship. No one enjoys being hurt but when you push people away, you just rob yourself of the connections that you can have with supportive people.

You can find hope again. I need you to get your fight back. Today is another day to take a leap of faith and reach out. You know you need help so please do not go another day without getting some support. It is time to come out of the pit. Try this again because your life matters. Every day we take the risk to talk to people, but we can grow from the experience. It is not wise to give up on yourself because of foolish actions from other people who did not appreciate you.

Isolation

      I remember having personal moments like these. I felt so exhausted from being hurt repeatedly by people I placed trust in. Guess what, I learned later in life that I did not have healthy boundaries. I had to learn how to advocate for myself and understand that it is okay to tell people **NO**. I also had to learn what healthy relationships with people looked like. Get moving again. Did you lose your desire to do the things you enjoy? Get your hobby back. Good fun is also good for your mental health.

God's Promise

Proverbs 18:24 (NKJV)

24 A man *who has* friends must himself be friendly,
But there is a friend *who* sticks closer than a brother.

Chapter Six
Extreme Loss

I remember in a three-year period losing over 20 loved ones! I cannot adequately describe the level of pain that I endured but I am grateful that I got through it. There were times I asked God, *"What did my family do to deserve all this back-to-back pain?"* Some of you can relate to this statement if you have been faced with tragedy or loss at an extreme level. I would not wish my past losses on my worst enemy at all! Losing one person is painful but what about repeatedly losing loved ones within months apart?

If you are in deep grief right now you can get through it. One of the most important things is to realize that there are support groups that can help you. **Grief Share** has a global network of groups that help people through a virtual platform or in person. Just google this network and you will see several options. The key is to remember that you are not alone. Losing a loved one is difficult and you may feel that you just cannot go on without that person. These are normal feelings but with the right help you can recover.

Some of you reading this may be grieving right now. I must confess that I had thoughts of giving up and wanting God to take me home early so I could be with my loved ones. I strongly felt this way when I lost my grandmother and one of my favorite uncles. Please know that it is important that you make positive contributions in life while you are here. One life ends but you can take all the lessons that you learned from your loved ones and apply it to your own life. This was a strategy that helped me cope with the pain and loss. I thought about my dear uncle who showed me the importance of a strong work ethic by the way he worked after retirement! I smiled when I remembered his lighthearted laughs, sharing a meal at the kitchen table and watching our favorite shows together. I decided that I would laugh more, work hard and cherish the moments that I spend with family and friends.

Extreme Loss

Has anyone ever told you to smile more? You know when you are in pain it is difficult to smile but when you think about happy times or funny moments with your loved ones, it will change your mood. Go ahead, think about a time when you had a deep belly laugh. Some of you are saying, "This is dumb". I get it, you don't feel like laughing right now but laughing is medicine for the soul. As I reflect on my past losses, I do remember people commenting on how serious my face was all the time. My face told a story of deep pain. I literally used to look in the mirror to practice smiling, but it was difficult a times because of the heaviness in my heart.

What do you do? First, stop trying to change how you feel around people and just be honest. You will attract the right ones who will stick around and support you in your healing journey. Yes, it can be annoying to have so many people tell you how to feel when you know how you feel at that moment! Don't blow up at them, just tell them you need some space and time to process the loss. It is true that you will feel there is no one who understands you. During those moments remember that God knows exactly how you feel.

Write your feelings on paper, make a poem or even sing an uplifting song. Whatever you decide to do, just release the hurt in a healthy way. I send my heartfelt condolences to all of you who lost loved ones and who are still walking through grief. As you read through this short book, you will find your heart feeling lighter and lighter. Keep going. If you must stop and cry for a moment, do it. It is okay to release those tears because that is part of your healing journey.

God's Promise

Psalm 16:11 (KJV)

11 Thou wilt shew me the path of life: in thy presence is fulness of joy; at thy right hand there are pleasures for evermore.

Chapter Seven
Toxic Media

Ask yourself this question, "*What are you feeding your mind with daily?*" One of the biggest problems in our society is the overload of negative information that is poured out through social media. Snap chat, Twitter, Tic Toc, Facebook, YouTube just to name a few. Take control over what you put in your mind. Have you ever watched something sad and depressing on social media that changed your entire mood for the rest of the day? Social media can be used for good purposes but if you are always watching unhealthy things, it is time to make a change.

If you are controlled by social media, you are in a danger zone. Some things that are posted are not reality. AI, known as *Artificial Intelligence*, has taken over social media! People tell lies on other people, alter photos and even post fake backgrounds to pretend they are somewhere else. Some post money, cars and even houses to garner likes. Following shallow people is not the way to heal your mind. Take a break from social media. You will find that you will be emotionally healthier and desire connections with humans. It is easy to fall into the trap of seeking attention, affirmation and popularity behind a screen.

We humans were made for community so we should not live our lives through technology. In addition to social media, television has become more bolder in normalizing sexual perversion, violence and crime. Watching horrific things can lead to mind battles like nightmares. Be mindful of the toxic things that you put in your mind because it will change the way you think. The next time you feel down, pick up your phone and call a friend instead of surfing the internet for answers from someone you don't know. An overconsumption of social media will place you in isolation which can lead to depression.

Never forget the power in hearing a voice or accepting a kind hug from a person when you are upset. I don't care how many emojis you send people through text; it will **NEVER** replace the power of being present. Think about the small things you can do to replace your time on social media or watching television. If you have hobby, go do it. It could be painting, running, skating, writing, singing, decorating, or collecting rare items. You owe it to yourself to wake up and enjoy your life again. Remember, your life matters. Repeat this phrase out loud: ***Your Life Matters.***

God's Promise

Romans 12:2 (KJV)

² And be not conformed to this world: but be ye transformed by the renewing of your mind, that ye may prove what is good, and acceptable, and perfect will of God.

Chapter Eight
Get Active Again

Take a quick inventory of your life right now. Do you find yourself hating your life after comparing yourself to others? It is best to avoid the comparison trap. Sometimes we see the best public presentation in others when there may be some trouble at home that they are hiding. Focus on yourself right now. Your life really does matter. When was the last time you took a walk in the park, flew a kite, or took an art class? Maybe you don't like any of those options, but there is something that you used to do.

Sometimes "life happens" and we stop everything enjoyable that we used to do.

Depression has a way of choking out the best of your hours, days, or years if you remain a captive. I have experienced this and felt at times there was no way out of my deep despair. I was wrong. I decided to make a list of all the enjoyable things I used to do and plan a time to do them again. What was your hobby? Some of you stopped doing things after certain people left your life. Your happiness cannot depend on another person.

I mentioned earlier that sitting and watching hours and hours of television or being glued to your cell phone is not healthy. Once you begin doing the things you loved you will find that you will connect with others more easily. Make new friends. It may feel awkward at first but get back out there and get active again. Make a list now and choose your top three activities. Set a date and time and take the bold step. Ready. Set. Go!

God's Promise

Psalm 118:24 (ESV)

24 This is the day that the Lord has made; let us rejoice and be glad in it.

Chapter Nine
Your Purpose

What do you envision yourself doing in five years? Have you ever been asked this from an employer and fumbled your way through it? It is the worst feeling when you have no idea where you're going. In life we can coast by and stay in the safe zone, or we can venture out to explore what is in us. Some people are going nowhere fast! One way to help you focus your life is to write down plans. Do you remember when I asked you to write down three things you enjoy doing to get active again?

Guess what, you can do that with your entire life! Companies have visions. When you work for an employer, you are supporting the company's vision. Why not create one for yourself? Life has been hard. Some of us were not born with a silver spoon in our mouths. I had some major hardships growing up, but at some point, I needed to release those negative feelings about my childhood and move on. It is time to value yourself and come out of the rut that you have been in for a long time. God created you for a special purpose. Sometimes you may not see it right away but do not get discouraged about it.

Create a vision board. It sounds deep, but it is not. Take out paper or some sticky notes and create goals that can be measurable with a timeframe. You may not accomplish everything in your projected time—and that's ok. Go back and review what was accomplished and set new dates. Your goals should reflect what you are most passionate about. Do you like to help others? What job can you do to foster this characteristic? Do you play an instrument? Set a goal to take lessons or use YouTube until you can pay someone. This is definitely a positive way to use YouTube. No more limiting yourself. Visions can keep your life on track and provide meaning. If you are married with children, you can set family goals. It can be something as simple as helping a teenager learn how to drive or having a fun family game night for bonding time. If you are a teenager who is reading this book, you can set a goal to reach out to a trusted adult to build a support network.

Once you get our eyes off what other people are doing, you can really find out what **YOU** need to do! You are not worthless. You are valued. Build your self-worth up by checking back in life. I know some of you lived your life fighting to survive with limited support, but it can change today. It starts with a vision. Your vision will improve your quality of life because you will finally have a clear purpose for your life.

God's Promise

Psalm 16:9 (ESV)

9 The heart of man plans his way, but the LORD establishes his steps.

Chapter Ten
True Friends

Everyone knows what it feels like to lose good friends and to have fake friends who are opportunists. I had both types in my life, but mostly opportunists compared to real friends. I learned over the years that people will try very hard to befriend you to examine you closely to find out what you know, who you know and how they can personally benefit. There is another popular quote that says, *"Show me your friends and I'll show you your future."*

Your inner circle tells a lot about who you really are. Unfortunately, there will be times that you will outgrow friends. If you are striving to be more and do more this will naturally happen. Do not view this as a bad thing but change is good. It happens when you decide to grow in every area of your life. **DO NOT** allow yourself to become stagnant. Let go of miserable or complacent people who always bring you down. These types of people will suck the energy out of you like a vampire. I have too many experiences to mention in this book on how people tried to pull me down because of their own unhappiness.

Sometime the heaviness your heart feels is because you are holding on to people that you must release from your life. Sure, everyone needs a friend, but it should not cost you your sanity! You will experience times when so call friends backstab you or even become jealous and envious of you. This is not the time to fight them, but it is a time to move on and **DO YOU**. You have a purpose to fulfill, and it is time to stop holding onto unhealthy relationships. Maybe you have anxiety about losing all your friends. When you begin to do things that you enjoy, you will begin to meet people with similar interests. **Your life matters.**

I know you want to hang with people who like you. So do I, but not if it costs me my peace. You may be pondering on how to identify true friends. People will always put on their best self when they first meet you but over time the mask will fall off! When seeking genuine friends, below are some questions to ask yourself:

- *Does this person respect my boundaries?*
- *Does this person allow me to feel seen and heard?*
- *Does this person always point out my flaws rather than encourage me?*
- *Does this person compete with everything I do?*
- *Does this person celebrate my successes or downplay them?*
- *Does this person get upset when I do things with other people?*
- *Does this person constantly gossip or make fun of other people?*

God's Promise

1 Corinthians 15:33 (NCV)

33 Do not be fooled: "Bad friends will ruin good habits."

A Prayer

Dear Lord,

Help me to see my value again and to understand that I have a purpose to fulfill. I admit that I have allowed too many negative things into my life and carried burdens that were never meant for me to carry. My broken heart needs healing and total restoration. Lord, send authentic and caring people in my life. I realize how important it is to live in community and not in isolation. I know there were several times that I checked out of life and just existed. I let go of this depression, bitterness and anger towards myself and people who failed me in my childhood. Today I am making a change to help myself. I am no longer looking for people or things to complete me. Today I get out of my cave and take a bold step to do something I enjoy. I also release toxic people and come out of this stagnant place. I declare that I am walking in my new season healed and whole. No more dumping my toxic baggage on others or comparing myself to people. I get up again because my life matters! Thankyou Lord for hearing my cry and touching my broken heart today. In the mighty name of Jesus, I pray. Amen.

Made in the USA
Columbia, SC
15 December 2024

49474156R00029